101

4th of July Jokes for Kids

Copyright 2019 by Hayden Fox - All rights reserved.

This document is geared towards providing exact and reliable information in regards to the topic and issue covered. The publication is sold with the idea that the publisher is not required to render an accounting, officially permitted, or otherwise, qualified services. If advice is necessary, legal or professional, a practiced individual in the profession should be ordered.

- From a Declaration of Principles which was accepted and approved equally by a Committee of the American Bar

Association and a Committee of Publishers and Associations.

In no way is it legal to reproduce, duplicate, or transmit any part of this document by either electronic means or in printed format. Recording of this publication is strictly prohibited and any storage of this document is not allowed unless with written permission from the publisher. All rights reserved.

The information provided herein is stated to be truthful and consistent, in that any liability, in terms of inattention or otherwise, by any usage or abuse of any policies, processes, or directions contained within is the solitary and utter responsibility of the recipient reader. Under no circumstances will any legal responsibility or blame be held against the publisher for any reparation, damages, or monetary loss due to the information herein, either directly or indirectly.

Respective authors and companies own all copyrights not held by the publisher.

The information herein is offered for informational purposes solely and is universal as so. The presentation of the information is without a contract or any type of guarantee assurance.

The trademarks that are used are without any consent, and the publication of the trademark is without permission or backing by the trademark owner. All trademarks and brands within this book are for clarifying purposes only and are owned by the owners themselves, not affiliated with this document.

What colonists told the most jokes?

Punsylvanians

What did one flag say to the other flag?

Nothing, it just waved!

What do you get when you cross Captain America with the Incredible Hulk?

The Star Spangled Banner

Why did the duck say bang?

Because he was a firequacker!

Why were the first Americans like ants?

Because they lived in colonies!

What protest by a group of dogs occurred in 1773?

The Boston Flea Party

What do you get when you cross a dinosaur with fireworks?

Dinomite

What was the American colonists' favorite tea?

Liberty

What was the most popular dance in early American history?

Indepen-dance

What was General Washington's favorite tree?

Infantry

Who was the funniest person in George Washington's army?

Laughayette

What do you eat on July 5th?

Independence Day old pizza

What quacks and betrays his country?

Beneduck Arnold

What happened as a result of the Stamp Act?

The Americans licked the British!

What's red, white, blue and black?

A bruised Uncle Sam!

Why isn't there a knock knock joke about America?

Because freedom rings!

What's the difference between a duck and George Washington?

One has a bill on his face while the other has his face on a bill!

Did you hear about the joke of Liberty Bell?

Yeah, it cracked me up!

What did the fuse say to the firecracker?

Let's join and pop it like it's hot!

What happened when the battery and firecracker were arrested?

One was charged and the other was let off!

What's red, white, blue and green?

A seasick Uncle Sam

What do you get if you cross the first signer of the Declaration of Independence with a rooster?

John Hancock-a-doodle-doo

What did one firecracker say to the other firecracker?

My pop's bigger than your pop!

What has feathers, webbed feet, and certain inalienable rights?

The Ducklaration of Independence

What do you get if you cross George Washington with cattle feed?

The Fodder of Our Country

Where was the Declaration of Independence signed?

At the bottom!

What do you get if you cross a patriot with a small curly-haired dog?

Yankee Poodle

Where did George Washington buy his hatchet?

At the chopping mall!

How is a healthy person like the United States?

They both have great constitutions!

What was the craziest battle of the Revolutionary War?

The Battle of Bonkers Hill

Where did George Washington keep his mice?

Mt. Vermin

Does Europe have a 4th of July?

Yes, it comes right after July 3rd!

What did the colonists wear to the Boston Tea Party?

Tea-shirts

Which famous person do you get when you make a wreath out of $100 bills?

Aretha Franklin

Was the Declaration of Independence signed in Philadelphia?

No, it was signed in ink!

Why did the British soldiers wear red coats?

So they could hide in the tomatoes!

What's red, white, blue and ugly?
The Revolutionary Warthog!

Why did Paul Revere ride from Boston to Lexington?
Because the horse was too heavy to carry

What's red, white, blue and green?

A patriotic pickle

What is Uncle Sam's favorite snack?

Fire-crackers

What did King George think of the American colonists?

He thought they were revolting!

How do Americans spend their 4th of July weekend?

Being stuck in traffic!

Which letter is the coolest on the 4th of July?

Iced T

What do couples do for fun on July 4th?

They go to an Indepen-Dance party!

What sport is played on July 4th?

American Flag Football

What do you call a snowman on July 4th?

A puddle

What treats do dads like on July 4th?

POPsicles

How do grizzlies stay cool on Independence Day?

They use bear conditioning!

What did Paul Revere say at the end of his ride?

I need a softer saddle!

Why did the British cross the Atlantic?

To get to the other tide!

What snack did the parrot want on the 4th of July?

Fire Crackers

What did the little firecracker say to the big firecracker?

Hey Pop!

Who gave Philadelphia the Liberty Bell?

A duck because it had a quack in it!

When is the best time to have a parade?

March

What do firemen eat with their soup?

Firecrackers

What's red, white, blue and green?

A patriotic turtle

Why did the duck say bang?

Because he was a fire quacker!

When's the 4th of July in England?

Between the 3rd and 5th!

What ghost haunted King George III?

The spirit of '76

What did the patriot put on his dry skin?

Revo-lotion

Why does Uncle Sam wear red, white and blue suspenders?

To hold up his pants!

What was a Patriot's favorite food during the war?

Chicken Catch-a-Tory

What would you get if you crossed Jon with King George in 1776?

King George the Nerd

Who is a dog's favorite Founding Father?

Bone Franklin

What is the cross between a dog and the first President?

George Washingtongue

What is a hungry boy's favorite picnic event?

The snack race

What did Washington say as he crossed the Delaware?

Next time I'm going to reserve a seat!

How did we win the battle of Trenton?

The enemy soldiers were Hessian around!

What is the cross between a monster and one of Washington's officers?

Baron von Steupid

What has four legs, a shiny nose, and fought for England?

Rudolph the Redcoat Reindeer!

What is the cross between a monster and a redcoat?

A bigger enemy

What cat warned about the British coming?

Paw Revere

What was Thomas Jefferson's favorite dessert?

Monti jello

Whose son helped write the Declaration of Indpendence?

Thomas Jeffer's son

What famous pig signed the Declaration of Independence?

John Hamcock

What's the cross between a bird of prey and a beagle?

A bald beagle

What is the cross between a colonial hairpiece and a teepee?

A powdered wigwam

What did the visitor say when he left the Statue of Liberty?

Keep in torch!

What's big, cracked, and carries your luggage?

The Liberty Bellhop

What's the cross between a monster and Yankee Doodle?

Yankee Doofus!

What's red, white, blue and black?

An injured Uncle Sam!

What's red, white and blue?

A strange candy cane

Why should you put sunscreen on your bananas on July 4th picnic?

Because they peel when they get a sunburn!

How can you tell the ocean is friendly on Independence Day?

It waves!

What did the bacon say to the tomato at the 4th of July picnic?

Lettuce get together!

Did you hear about the 4th of July picnic without beverages?

It was soda pressing!

Who came to the 4th of July picnic but wasn't invited?

The ants

Why should you do research before buying fireworks?

To get the best bang for your buck!

Why are fireworks so cool on the 4th of July?

Because they're lit!

What did the lightning say to the fireworks on July 4th?

You stole my thunder!

Did you pass your fireworks exam?

Yeah with flying colors!

Why do people use fireworks on July 4th?

Because fire works!

What march would you play at a jungle parade?

Tarzan stripes forever!

Why does Trump want to ban the sale of pre-shredded cheese?

To make America grate again!

If Canadians speak "English eh" then what do Americans speak?

English B

What did Tennessee?

Same as Arkansas!

What is Donald Trump's favorite instrument?

The trumpet

Why can't you hunt a bald eagle in America?

It's ill-eagle!

Did you hear about the 4th of July pizza joke?

Never mind it was too cheesy!

What happened when the American broke his arm on July 4th?

He went broke!

What American president was the least guilty?

Lincoln because he was in a cent!

Thank you for reading!

www.ingramcontent.com/pod-product-compliance
Lightning Source LLC
Chambersburg PA
CBHW071254070526
44583CB00017B/2472